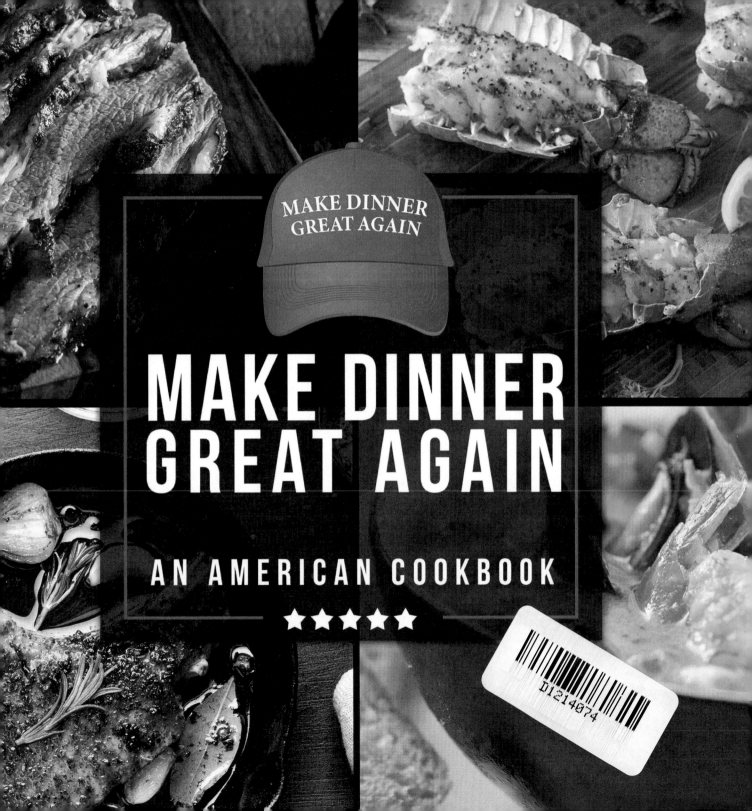

MAKE DINNER GREAT AGAIN

MAKE DINNER GREAT AGAIN

AN AMERICAN COOKBOOK

★★★★★

D1214074

MAKE DINNER GREAT AGAIN

AN AMERICAN COOKBOOK

★ ★ ★ ★ ★

BY: ANNA KONIK

Buffalo Bleu Chicken Dip

Starters

★★★★★

Caprese Salad	6
Pear and Ricotta Bruschetta	7
Buffalo Bleu Chicken Dip	8
Bacon, Brie & Onion Bites	10
Shrimp Ceviche	11
Bacon & Cheese Jalapeño Boats	12
Crab Au Gratin Dip	13
Street Corn Dip	14
Bacon Wrapped Chicken Bites	15

Caprese Salad

Ingredients:

- 5 Large Heirloom Tomatoes
- 1 lb. Fresh Mozzarella, sliced
- 1 bunch of Fresh Basil Leaves
- 1 tsp. Italian Seasoning
- 1 tsp. Himalayan Sea Salt
- 1 tsp. Fresh Cracked Black Pepper
- ½ tsp. Dried Rosemary
- 3 tbsp. Balsamic Vinegar

Instructions:

1. To begin, slice the heirloom tomatoes into large slices, about ¼ inch thick. Alternate tomato slice, mozzarella slice and a basil leaf in a circle on a serving plate.
2. Right before serving, drizzle lightly with balsamic vinegar and season with fresh salt, pepper, Italian seasoning and dried rosemary.
3. Serve immediately and enjoy!

Pear and Ricotta Bruschetta

Ingredients:

- 1 Loaf Sourdough Bread
- 1 Pear, sliced
- ⅓ cup Walnuts, crushed
- 2 cups Ricotta Cheese
- ¼ cup Honey
- Fresh Herbs, for garnish

Instructions:

1. To begin, slice the sourdough loaf into ½ inch thick slices. Spoon about ¼ cup ricotta onto each slice and lightly smear, leaving chunks. Rinse and dry the pear, then slice it into ¼ inch thick slices.

2. Top the ricotta with about 3-4 slices of pear, sprinkle crushed walnuts on top and drizzle with honey.

3. Serve immediately and enjoy!

Buffalo Bleu Chicken Dip

Ingredients:

- 6 (6 oz.) Chicken Breast Fillets, cut into chunks
- 2 (8 oz.) pkg. Cream Cheese (room temperature)
- 1 cup Bleu Cheese Dressing
- 1 cup Buffalo Sauce
- 1½ cup Cheddar Cheese, shredded
- ½ cup Bleu Cheese Crumbles
- 2 tbsp. Olive Oil
- Himalayan Sea Salt & Black Pepper
- Fresh Parsley, for garnish
- French Baguette, sliced

Instructions:

1. To begin, preheat the oven to 350°F. Arrange the sliced baguette slices on a baking sheet and drizzle olive oil, salt, and pepper on them. Bake for 13-15 minutes, or until golden and crispy.
2. In a large skillet over medium-high heat the olive oil. Add the chunks of chicken to the skillet, tossing occasionally until cooked through, about 7-10 minutes. Remove and place on a cutting board. Chop the chicken into smaller pieces.
3. In a large mixing bowl, add the cream cheese, bleu cheese dressing, bleu cheese crumbles (reserving some for garnish), buffalo sauce and 1 cup cheddar. Once mixed, toss in the chicken to the bowl and mix.
4. Transfer mixture to a deep dish pan and spread evenly. Spread remains cheddar cheese on top and bake for 25-30 minutes until bubbly and golden. Remove from heat, garnish with remaining bleu cheese crumbles and fresh parsley. Serve with crostinis and enjoy!

Chicken Skewers with Tzatziki Sauce

Ingredients:

- 4 (6 oz.) Chicken Breast Fillets
- 8-10 Wooden Skewers
- 4 Garlic Cloves, minced
- 2 Lemons
- ¼ cup Red Wine Vinegar
- ⅓ cup Grapeseed Oil
- 1 tbsp. Thyme
- 1 tbsp. Oregano
- 2 tbsp. Dill Weed
- 14 oz. Greek Yogurt
- ½ English Cucumber, diced
- Himalayan Sea Salt and Black Pepper

Instructions:

1. To begin, cut the chicken into 1-inch pieces and set aside. In a medium bowl, mix the red wine vinegar, grapeseed oil, juice of 1 lemon, garlic, oregano, and thyme. Add the chicken into the bowl and toss until fully coated. Cover and let marinate for at least 1 hour. Preheat oven to 450°F.

2. Once marinated, use the wooden skewers to thread chicken making sure that they are lightly touching. Repeat until all skewers are full and place on baking sheet. Bake for 5 minutes then remove lower heat to 350°F, and flip the skewers. Place back in the oven for 10-12 minutes or until cooked through.

3. While chicken is cooking, prepare your sauce. In a small bowl mix the juice of 1 lemon, greek yogurt, dill, cucumber and a pinch of black pepper. Keep cold until ready to serve.

4. Serve chicken on skewers with the tzatziki sauce and lemon wedges. Enjoy!

Bacon, Brie & Onion Bites

Ingredients:

- French Baguette
- 6 slices Bacon
- 1 block of Brie
- 4 cups Yellow Onions, sliced thinly
- 1 ½ cups Apple Cider Vinegar
- 2 tsp. Thyme Leaves
- Himalayan Sea Salt and Pepper
- ¼ White Wine Vinegar
- ¼ cup Brown Sugar
- 1 tsp. Ground Ginger

Instructions:

1. Preheat oven to 350°F. While it preheats, cut the baguette into diagonal slices and place them on a baking sheet. Brush both sides with olive oil, sprinkle black pepper and Himalayan sea salt to season. Bake until golden, 15 to 20 minutes. Remove from heat and allow to cool.

2. While crostinis bake, heat a large saucepan on medium-high heat. Add bacon to pan and cook until lightly crispy. Remove from heat and let cool. Using the excess fat in the pan add in the onions. Lower heat to medium, stir occasionally until onions softened.

3. Chop bacon into ¼ inch pieces and add it into the pan with the onions. Add in the ACV, thyme, a pinch of salt and pepper, brown sugar, and ginger into pan.

4. Leave uncovered and cook until liquid is almost non-existent. Reduce heat to low and allow onions to cook until rich brown color. Add ⅓ cup water if starts to become too dry.

5. Once it reaches the desired color, remove from heat to let cool. Slice brie into thin slices and place on top of crostinis. Top with bacon, onion marmalade and serve!

Shrimp Ceviche

Ingredients:

- 1 lb. raw Shrimp (deveined and peeled)
- 8 Limes
- 1 cup Tomato, chopped
- ½ cup White Onion, chopped
- 1 Jalapeño, finely diced
- ½ cup Cilantro, chopped
- Sea Salt and Black Pepper
- 1 tsp. Cayenne

Instructions:

1. To begin, juice 4 limes and combine with the shrimp. Cover and place in refrigerator for 14-16 minutes (depending on the size of shrimp). In a separate bowl, juice the other 4 limes, chopped tomato, onion, jalapeño, cilantro, and cayenne.
2. Check on shrimp, once fully pink, remove from fridge and combine with the rest of the ingredients. Add sea salt and pepper to taste.
3. Transfer ceviche to a glass bowl, serve with tortilla chips and enjoy!

Bacon & Cheese Jalapeño Boats

Instructions:

1. To begin, cut the jalapeños in half, lengthwise and remove the seeds. In a large skillet over medium-high heat, add the bacon and cook until crispy, about 3-5 minutes per side (depending on the thickness). Remove from skillet and place on paper towel to drain excess oil. Once dry, dice the bacon into small pieces.

2. Preheat the oven to 350°F. In a medium bowl, combine the following: 3/4 cup cheddar cheese, cream cheese, garlic powder, 3/4 of the crushed bacon, and sea salt. Mix well until smooth. Arrange the peppers on non-stick baking sheet and begin spooning about ¼ cup into each jalapeño half. Repeat until all jalapeños are filled.

3. Use the remaining ¼ cup of cheddar cheese to top the jalapeños. Bake for 15-20 minutes, until cheese is melted and bubbly. Remove from oven and transfer to serving plate.

4. Garnish with reserved bacon pieces and serve immediately. Enjoy!

Ingredients:

- 6 Jalapeño Peppers
- 5 slices Bacon
- 1 cup Cheddar Cheese, shredded
- 6 oz. Cream Cheese, room temperature
- ½ tsp. Garlic Powder
- ½ tsp. Sea Salt

Crab Au Gratin Dip

Ingredients:

- 1 lb. Jumbo Lump Crab Meat
- ½ Yellow Onion, chopped
- 2 Garlic Cloves, minced
- 4 oz. Cream Cheese softened
- 3/4 cup Half & Half
- 1 ½ stick Butter, melted
- 1 cup shredded Cheddar Cheese
- 1 cup shredded Gruyére Cheese
- ½ tsp. Cayenne Pepper
- 2 tbsp. Flour
- 1 tbsp. Lemon Juice
- Sea Salt and Black Pepper, to taste

Instructions:

1. To begin, preheat oven to 350°F. In a large skillet over medium-high heat, melt the butter. Add in the garlic and onions and cook, stirring occasionally, until translucent. About 5 minutes. Add in the flour to the skillet and stir, do not let flour brown. About 2 minutes.

2. Add in the half & half, stirring constantly. Stir in the lemon juice, cayenne, salt, and pepper. Keep stirring to create creamy soup thickness. Add water if it becomes too thick, 1 tbsp. at a time. Remove from heat and add in the cheddar cheese, gruyére, and cream cheese. Blend well by folding over until completely melted.

3. Divide the crabmeat among 3-4 oven-proof bowls. Pour the cheese sauce over the crab, evenly. Top with additional cheese or leftover crab.

4. Place in oven and allow to bake for about 13-15 minutes, depending on your bowls. Once bubbly, switch to broil for 4-5 minutes. Remove from oven and serve with bread or chips. Enjoy!

Street Corn Dip

Ingredients:

- 3 cups Sweet Corn
- 1 ½ tbsp. Olive Oil
- ⅓ cup Cotija Cheese
- 2 tsp. fresh Lime Juice
- ⅓ cup Mayonnaise
- Himalayan Sea Salt and Black Pepper
- ⅓ cup Red Onion, diced
- ⅓ cup Cilantro Leaves, chopped
- 2 tsp. Paprika or Chili Powder
- 1 Garlic Clove, minced

Instructions:

1. To begin, heat olive oil on medium-high heat. Add the corn and stir occasionally to achieve a slightly charred flavor. Remove from heat. Allow cooling for 5-10 minutes. In a medium bowl, mix the following: corn, mayonnaise, lime juice, garlic, red onion, and paprika together.

2. Add cilantro, Cotija cheese, salt, and pepper to season and lightly toss. Serve in chilled bowl with cilantro to garnish. Serve with warm tortilla chips! Enjoy!

Bacon Wrapped Chicken Bites

Instructions:

1. To begin, preheat the oven to 350°F. Cut the chicken into small pieces, about 1 inch thick. Pat dry with the paper towels and transfer to a medium bowl. Season with garlic powder, cayenne pepper, salt, black pepper, and red pepper flakes. Toss to coat, it should be a very light coat.

2. Cut the strips of bacon into thirds. In a small bowl, mix the brown sugar and chili powder. Have a greased pan ready. One at a time, wrap the chicken piece with bacon and secure with a toothpick. Take the wrapped chicken and coat it in the brown sugar mixture and onto the pan. Repeat until all chicken is wrapped and coated.

3. Bake for 20-25 minutes for regular bacon or 30-45 minutes for thick-cut bacon. Remove from pan, place in a bowl and serve hot. Enjoy!

Ingredients:

- 4 (6 oz.) Chicken Breast Fillets
- 1 (16 oz.) pkg. Bacon
- 2 tbsp. Chili Powder
- 2/3 cup Brown Sugar
- ½ tsp. Garlic Powder
- ½ tsp. Cayenne Powder
- ½ tsp. Sea Salt
- ½ tsp. Black Pepper
- ½ tsp. Red Pepper Flakes
- Toothpicks or Small Forks, for serving
- Himalayan Sea Salt and Black Pepper

Italian Spaghetti & Meatballs

Meals

★★★★★

Herb Roasted Whole Chicken

Ingredients:

- 1 Whole Chicken
- 6 tbsp. Butter, melted
- 1 Lemon
- 1 Head of Garlic
- 2 tbsp. Italian Seasoning
- 5 fresh Thyme Sprigs
- 5 fresh Rosemary Sprigs
- Sea Salt and Black Pepper, to taste

Instructions:

1. To begin, preheat the oven to 425°F. Using paper towels, pat the chicken dry. Cut one lemon and the garlic head in half, horizontally. Place the lemon halves, garlic head, thyme, rosemary and a pinch of salt inside the chicken cavity. Place the stuffed chicken in a baking dish.

2. Brush half of the butter all over the skin of the chicken. Sprinkle with Italian seasoning and any leftover thyme or rosemary. Bake the chicken for 20 minutes.

3. Remove from oven, brush the rest of the butter all over the chicken and place back into the oven for an additional 25-30 minutes. Remove from oven, garnish with extra herbs and enjoy!

Cast Iron Pork Chops

Ingredients:

- 2 Pork Loin Rib Chops (center cut), room temperature
- ¼ cup Dry White Wine
- 4 tbsp. Butter
- 2 Thyme Sprigs
- 2 Rosemary sprigs
- 2 tbsp. Sugar
- 2 tbsp. Sea Salt
- 1 tsp. Black Pepper
- 1 tsp. Dried Parsley
- 3 Bay Leaves
- 3 Garlic Cloves

Instructions:

1. To begin, season the pork chops with sugar, salt and black pepper on both sides. Let marinate for at least 1 hour, then remove from fridge and let it come to room temperature.

2. Preheat the oven to 425°F. Heat a large skillet over medium-high heat and add 2 tbsp. butter once hot. Use a spoon to spread it so it does not burn and add the pork chops, sear them for 30-60 seconds on each side. Once seared, put them in the oven for 5-6 minutes.

3. Remove from oven and put the pork chops on a cutting board. Using the same skillet, add the remaining butter and white wine. Scrape the bottom browned bits and let the liquid reduce by half. Reduce heat to low and add in the rosemary, thyme, garlic cloves, bay leaves, and parsley into the skillet. Stir to combine well and remove from heat.

4. Place the pork chops back in the skillet, turning to cover in the herb butter. Spoon extra butter on top and serve immediately. Enjoy!

Mongolian Beef

Ingredients:

- 1 ½ lb. Flank Steak
- 3 Garlic Cloves, minced
- 3/4 cup Brown Sugar
- 1 cup Vegetable Oil
- ½ tsp. Red Pepper Flakes
- ½ cup Soy Sauce (Low Sodium)
- 2/4 cup Water
- 4-6 Scallion Stalks, cut diagonally (1-inch pieces)
- ½ cup Cornstarch
- 2 tsp. Fresh Ginger, minced
- 1 tsp. Onion Powder
- ½ tsp. Sea Salt
- ½ tsp. Black Pepper

Instructions:

1. To begin, heat 1 tbsp. vegetable oil in a saucepan over medium heat. Add the minced garlic and ginger, sauté for about 1 minute. Add the following: water, soy sauce, onion powder, and brown sugar. Bring to a boil, then reduce heat to allow to simmer for 10-12 minutes.

2. While the sauce simmers, prepare your steak by cutting it into ¼ inch slices, cutting diagonally. If pieces are too long, cut in half. Once completely cut, put in a medium bowl and toss with cornstarch to cover completely and let sit for 10 minutes.

3. In a large pan, heat remaining vegetable oil. Once hot, cook the beef in batches for 2-3 minutes each, flipping throughout. Remove from oil and transfer to sauce. Heat on medium for an additional 1-2 minutes to cover in sauce.

4. Disperse among plates, garnish with red pepper flakes and chopped scallion. Enjoy!

Seared Scallops with Asparagus

Instructions:

1. To begin, in a large skillet over medium-high heat, add in 1 tbsp. of olive oil. Add the asparagus and cook until tender, 4-5 minutes. Transfer to a plate.

2. Dry the scallops with a paper towel and lightly sprinkle sea salt and black pepper. Using the same skillet, add in another tbsp. of olive oil and half of the scallops. Cook until lightly golden, 3-4 minutes per side.

3. Transfer scallops to a plate and repeat with the remaining scallops. Once cooked and set aside, add in the white wine to the skillet. Bring to a boil and gently scrape the browned bits off the bottom of the pan, 3-4 minutes.

4. Once the sauce has reduced, heat on low and add in the butter one tablespoon at a time. Toss the asparagus in the butter then plate immediately. Add scallops on top, spoon sauce and garnish with microgreens. Enjoy!

Ingredients:

- 1 ½ lbs. Scallops
- 3 tbsp. Olive Oil
- 1 lb. Asparagus
- ⅓ cup Dry White Wine
- 4 tbsp. Butter
- 1 Garlic Clove, minced
- Sea Salt and Black Pepper, to taste
- Microgreens, for garnish

Italian Stuffed Portobello Mushrooms

Ingredients:

- 4 large Portobello Mushrooms
- 2 tbsp. Olive Oil
- ¼ cup Breadcrumbs
- 1 Garlic Cloves, minced
- ½ tsp. Sea Salt
- ½ tsp. Black Pepper
- 1 tsp. Italian Seasoning
- 1 tbsp. Tamari
- ½ cup Mozzarella Cheese, shredded
- ¼ cup Walnuts, finely chopped
- ½ Sweet Onion, chopped
- ¼ cup Vegetable Broth
- 1 Lemon
- 2 tbsp. Fresh Parsley, chopped

Instructions:

1. To begin, preheat the oven to 350°F. Clean the mushrooms and dry with a paper towel. Remove the stems and dice them, set aside. In a large skillet over medium-high heat, heat the olive oil. Add the garlic, onions, and mushroom stems and sauté for 2-3 minutes.

2. Add in the juice of one lemon, breadcrumbs, sea salt, black pepper, Italian seasoning, Tamari, and walnuts. Add the broth on top and reduce to medium heat, cook until most of the liquid is dissolved, stirring occasionally.

3. Carefully, one mushroom cap at a time, take the mushroom and spoon the skillet mixture into it until all four mushrooms are evenly filled. Place on a non-stick baking sheet, filling side up. Top with mozzarella cheese and bake for 18-20 minutes.

4. Plate and garnish with parsley, enjoy!

Mozzarella Stuffed Turkey Meatballs

Ingredients:

- 2 lbs. Ground Turkey
- 8 oz. Fresh Mozzarella Pearls (2 ½ g.)
- 4 Garlic Cloves, minced
- ½ Yellow Onion, diced
- ½ tsp. Red Pepper Flakes
- 1 Egg, beaten
- 2 tsp. Dried Oregano
- 2 tbsp. Italian Seasoning
- ½ tsp. Sea salt
- 3 tbsp. Tomato Paste
- 1 tbsp. Olive Oil
- 1 cup Panko Breadcrumbs
- Fresh Parsley, for garnish

Instructions:

1. To begin, preheat the oven to 375°F. In a large bowl, mix the ground turkey, egg, garlic, onion, breadcrumbs, tomato paste, oregano, Italian seasoning, and sea salt. Mix well and start creating meatballs about 2 inches thick.

2. Have a greased baking dish ready. Take one meatball at a time and place 2-3 mozzarella pearls directly into the center, then roll to close the meatball back up. Repeat until all meatballs are mozzarella stuffed. Place in the baking dish.

3. Bake for 30-33 minutes, or until cooked through. Remove from oven. To garnish, sprinkle the red pepper flakes on top and add fresh parsley. Serve straight from the dish. Enjoy!

Salmon Patties

Ingredients:

- 1 lb. Wild Salmon (no skin)
- ⅓ cup Panko Breadcrumbs
- 6 Hatch Chiles, chopped
- ½ Red Onion, diced
- 2 tbsp. Cilantro, chopped
- 2 tbsp. Olive Oil
- 1 tbsp. Paprika
- ½ tsp. Garlic Powder
- ½ tsp. Cayenne (adjust to taste)
- 2 tbsp. Grated Parmesan
- Himalayan Sea Salt and Black Pepper
- ¼ cup Mayonnaise

Instructions:

1. To begin, place salmon chunks in a medium bowl and begin breaking up into smaller pieces using a fork. Once fairly small chunks, add in the hatch chiles, red onion, cilantro, garlic powder, paprika, and cayenne. Mix well, add in the mayo and breadcrumbs until you get a consistency that will hold it together. Form the patties to your desired size and place aside.
2. Heat a medium skillet on medium heat, add olive oil. Place patties about 1 inch apart and let cook, covered for about 6 minutes on each side. Once it is lightly crispy on the exterior, remove from heat.
3. Serve over cabbage, in a burger bun, or as is! Enjoy!

Coconut Shrimp

Ingredients:

- 1 lb. raw large Shrimp, peeled (tails attached)
- 3/4 cup Panko Breadcrumbs
- 1 cup Coconut Flakes
- ¼ cup Canola Oil
- 2 Brown Eggs, beaten
- ½ tbsp. Paprika
- ½ tsp. Sea Salt
- ⅓ cup All-purpose Flour
- 1 Garlic Clove, pressed
- Cocktail Sauce

Instructions:

1. To begin, preheat oven to 350°F. On a baking sheet, spread out the panko and coconut flakes and toast in oven, stirring occasionally for about 6-8 minutes. Remove from oven, transfer to a bowl and raise the temperature to 450°F.

2. Replace the baking sheet and pour the canola oil, evenly spreading it all across. Set aside and grab two additional bowls. In one of the bowls, add the eggs and pressed garlic, beat well. In the other bowl, mix the flour, paprika, and salt.

3. Dip the shrimp in the flour mixture, proceeding to the eggs and ending with the toasted coconut mixture. Place the ready shrimp on the oiled sheet, once done place shrimp in the oven for 6-8 minutes, until they are a light pink color. Serve with cocktail sauce and enjoy!

Oven-Roasted BBQ Brisket

Ingredients:

- 4-5 lbs. Beef Brisket
- 1 cup BBQ Sauce
- 2 cups Beef Stock
- ⅓ cup Brown Sugar
- 2 tsp. Dry Mustard
- 2 tsp. Worcestershire Sauce
- 2 tsp. Chili Powder
- 2 tbsp. Sea Salt
- 1 tbsp. Smoked Paprika
- 1 tbsp. Black Pepper
- 1 tbsp. Onion Powder
- 1 tbsp. Garlic Powder

Instructions:

1. To begin, preheat the oven to 350°F. Cut any excess fat from the bottom of the brisket. In a bowl mix the following: brown sugar, dry mustard, chili powder, sea salt, paprika, black pepper, onion powder, and garlic powder. Rub the Worcestershire sauce all over the brisket. Then use the dry rub to completely season it on all sides.

2. Put the brisket in a baking dish with the fat cap, side-up. Roast, uncovered for about an hour. Remove from oven and pour the beef stock on top of the beef brisket, until there is about ½ inch in the pan. Add water, if needed. Reduce temperature to 275°F and cover with 2 layers of foil. Continue roasting for 3 hours. Remove the foil, brush the BBQ sauce all over the brisket and roast uncovered for an additional hour.

3. Remove from pan and let cool on a cutting board for about 10-15 minutes. Using a sharp knife, cut thin slices about ¼ inch thick. Serve and enjoy!

Simple Turkey Tacos

Ingredients:

- 1 ½ lb. Ground Turkey (Lean)
- 1 cup Red Onion, diced
- 2 Garlic Cloves, minced
- 1 tbsp. Olive Oil
- 2 tsp. Paprika
- 1 tsp. Chili Powder
- ½ tsp. Cinnamon
- ½ tsp. Black Pepper
- ½ tsp. Sea Salt
- 1 tbsp. Tomato Paste
- ¼ cup Water
- 6-8 (6-inch) Corn Tortillas

For the Lime Cream Sauce:

- ¼ cup Sour Cream
- 3 tbs. Mayonnaise
- 2 Limes, zest only
- 1 tbsp. Fresh Lime Juice

Instructions:

1. To begin, heat a medium saucepan over medium-high heat. Add the olive oil, garlic, and red onion. Cook for 2-3 minutes, until fragrant. Add in the ground turkey and cook for 8-10 minutes, stirring throughout.

2. While the turkey cooks, whisk together the sour cream, mayonnaise, rest of the zest, sea salt, and 1 lime juiced in a small bowl. Set aside in a cool place.

3. Add in the tomato paste, water, paprika, chili powder, cinnamon, black pepper, and sea salt. Mix well. Using a separate medium pan, heat over medium-high heat and cook tortillas about 15-30 seconds each side.

4. Scoop the turkey into the tortillas and drizzle with the lime cream sauce. Add avocado if desired. Enjoy!

Roasted Eggplant with Lemon-Yogurt and Pomegranate

Ingredients:

- 2 Whole Eggplants
- ½ cup Pomegranate Seeds
- 1 tsp. Fresh Parsley, chopped (additional for garnish)
- 3 Garlic Cloves, minced
- ½ cup Plain Greek Yogurt
- 2 tbsp. Walnuts, chopped
- 2 tbsp. Olive Oil
- 1 tbsp. Lemon Juice
- 1 tsp. Lemon Zest
- 1 tsp. Sea Salt
- ½ tsp. Onion Powder
- ½ tsp. Cumin
- ½ tsp. Black Pepper

Instructions:

1. To begin, carefully, cut the eggplant into 4 slices, lengthwise. Try to keep them all about the same thickness. In a small bowl, mix the following: parsley, garlic, sea salt, onion powder, cumin, and black pepper. Brush 1 tbsp. olive oil on both sides of the eggplant slices then season on both sides.

2. Place them flat on a cast iron skillet, top with foil, then top with another pan so it presses them down. Keep the stacked pans over medium-high heat and allow to roast for about 18-20 minutes, until tender.

3. While the eggplant roasts, combine the lemon juice, lemon zest, greek yogurt and a sprinkle of sea salt in a bowl.

4. Remove from oven and evenly divide among 4 plates. Top each eggplant slice with 1 tbsp. of lemon yogurt mixture, 1 tsp. pomegranate seeds (more if desired) and fresh parsley! Enjoy!

Italian Spaghetti & Meatballs

Ingredients:

- 1 lb. Ground Beef, Lean
- 4 Garlic Cloves, minced
- 12 oz. Spaghetti
- ¼ cup Parmesan Cheese
- ½ cup Mozzarella Cheese, shredded
- ⅓ cup Italian Seasoned Breadcrumbs
- 1 Egg, beaten
- 1 tbsp. Olive Oil
- 24 oz. Traditional Marinara Sauce
- Fresh Parsley, for garnish

Instructions:

1. To begin, preheat oven to 400°F. Prepare a non-stick or greased baking sheet. In a large mixing bowl, combine the ground beef, egg, garlic, breadcrumbs, and mozzarella. Mix well with your hands.

2. Use an ice cream scoop or your hands, portion about ¼ cup of meatball mixture and roll into a ball. Repeat until all meat is used and place on the baking sheet. Bake for 15 minutes then remove.

3. While the meatballs cook, heat a large pot of water with a pinch of salt. Add the spaghetti and let cook for 16-18 minutes, or until al dente.

4. Heat a large skillet over medium-high heat and add in the olive oil. Then add the marinara sauce. Reduce heat to a simmer. Add in the meatballs and let simmer for 8-10 minutes.

5. Drain the spaghetti and keep ¼ cup of pasta water. Add the pasta, pasta water and a pinch of salt. Mix well to coat the pasta.

6. Evenly divide into bowls, garnish with parmesan cheese and fresh parsley. Serve with more sauce, if desired. Enjoy!

Skirt Steak with Bleu Cheese Sauce

Ingredients:

- 1 lb. Skirt Steak
- 3 Garlic Cloves, minced
- 1 lb. Asparagus
- 3 tbsp. Olive Oil
- ½ cup Dry Red Wine
- 1 tsp. Chives, chopped
- 2 tbsp. Shallots, chopped
- ½ cup Sour Cream
- 2 oz. (about ½ cup) Bleu Cheese Crumbles, room temperature
- 2 tsp. Sea Salt
- 1 tsp. Black Pepper

Instructions:

1. To begin, create the marinade. In a baking dish, mix the following: red wine, garlic cloves, 1 tsp. sea salt and black pepper. Mix well then add the skirt steak, flipping to cover. Marinate for at least 2 hours, turning the steak halfway through.

2. Preheat your broiler. Once ready, broil the steak on the closest rack for 4-6 minutes per side. While the steak broils, get your bleu cheese sauce ready!

3. In a saucepan, over medium-high heat add 2 tbsp. olive oil and shallots. Sauté until softened, 1-2 minutes. Add in the white wine, and bring to a simmer until about half of the liquid has evaporated. Add in the sour cream, salt, and pepper. Mix well and slowly stir in the bleu cheese crumbles, stir until smooth.

4. In another skillet over medium-high heat, heat the remaining olive oil. Add in the asparagus, tossing occasionally and cook for 8-10 minutes, until cooked through.

5. Remove skirt steak from oven, transfer to cutting board and cut into ¼ inch pieces. Top with bleu cheese sauce and fresh chives. Serve with asparagus and enjoy!

Lemon Garlic Scampi with Shrimp

Ingredients:

- 1 ½ lb. large Shrimp (deveined)
- 8 oz. Angel Hair Spaghetti
- 4 Garlic Cloves, minced
- 3 Lemons
- 1 cup Virgin Olive Oil
- ½ cup grated Parmesan Cheese
- 1 cup fresh Parsley, chopped
- Himalayan Sea Salt and Black Pepper

Instructions:

1. To begin, zest 2 lemons and add zest into a medium bowl. Toss together with shrimp, ⅓ cup olive oil, parsley, and minced garlic. Set aside to marinate for at least 25 minutes, room temperature.
2. While marinating, bring a large pot of water to boil (add a pinch of sea salt). Once boiling, add spaghetti and cook for about 8-10 minutes, until tender. Remove and drain spaghetti, keeping 1 cup of spaghetti water.
3. While spaghetti cooks, heat a large skillet on medium-high heat and add shrimp to saucepan. Make sure they are all even and turn over after about 2-3 minutes. Once cooked transfer shrimps to a bowl.
4. In a small bowl, combine ½ cup olive oil, lemon juice of 2 lemons and the parmesan cheese. Combine the drained spaghetti and lemon-cheese mixture in the skillet and toss thoroughly. Add a little bit of spaghetti water at a time. Add in the parsley, sea salt, and pepper for taste.
5. Plate evenly and garnish with fresh lemon zest and parmesan cheese. Enjoy!

Fish Tacos with Cabbage Slaw

Ingredients:

- 1 lb. Cod Fillets
- 3 Limes
- 1 tbsp. Paprika
- 2 tbsp. Ground Cumin
- 3 Garlic Cloves, minced
- ¼ cup Soy Sauce (Low Sodium)
- ¼ cup fresh Orange Juice
- 8 (6 in.) Flour Tortillas
- 1 Avocado
- Himalayan Sea Salt and Black Pepper
- 2 tbsp. Chopped Cilantro
- ½ Green Onion, sliced
- 2 cups Red and Green Cabbage, finely shredded

For the Lime Cream Sauce:

- ¼ cup Sour Cream
- 3 tbs. Mayonnaise
- 2 Limes, zest only
- 1 tbsp. Fresh Lime Juice

Instructions:

1. To begin, combine fresh orange juice, ½ of the lime zest, juice of 1 lime, garlic, and soy sauce in a small bowl. Pour into a Ziploc bag and add fish, let marinate for 20-30 minutes in the refrigerator. At this time preheat oven to 425°F.
2. While marinating, whisk together the sour cream, mayonnaise, rest of the zest, sea salt, and 1 lime juiced in a small bowl. Set aside in a cool place.
3. Grab a large bowl and add the 2 cups of shredded cabbage, cilantro, green onion, and red onion. Toss thoroughly and place in the refrigerator until ready to serve.
4. Remove the fish and place on a non-stick baking sheet. Bake for about 10-12 minutes, until the fish is flaky and cooked through. While cooking, heat a large skillet on medium-high and warm each tortilla for 1-2 minutes on each side. Remove from heat and place in a warm towel to keep warm.
5. Transfer the fish to a plate and gently break into pieces with a fork. Divide the fish evenly on the tortillas, top with the cabbage slaw, lime cream sauce, and avocado. Serve and enjoy!

Stuffed Bell Peppers

Ingredients:

- 5 large Bell Peppers (any colors)
- 1 lb. Ground Beef (lean)
- 16 oz. Fire Roasted Tomatoes, diced
- ½ cup Long Grain Rice
- ½ cup Yellow Onion, chopped
- 3 Garlic Cloves, minced
- 1 tbsp. Olive Oil
- 1 tsp. Sea Salt
- 1 tsp. Black Pepper
- ½ tsp. Paprika
- 1 cup Cheddar Cheese, shredded
- 1 tsp. Parsley, additional for garnish

Instructions:

1. To begin, wash and dry your bell peppers. Cut the tops off, about 1 inch from the stem. Discard of the seeds and membrane, holding onto any pepper pieces from the tops. Chop remaining pepper tops and set aside. Boil a pot of water, once boiling add the peppers to cook for about 4-5 minutes. Remove from water and invert to drain.

2. Preheat the oven to 350°F. In a medium skillet over medium-high heat, heat the olive oil. Add in the garlic and onion and cook for 1-2 minutes, until fragrant. Add in the beef and chopped pepper remains. Cook for 6-8 minutes.

3. While meat cooks, bring a small pot to boil. Add in the rice and cook, covered for 10-12 minutes, until soft. Remove from heat and set aside.

4. Add in the drained tomatoes, salt, pepper, paprika and parsley to the meat. Mix well. Add in the rice to the beef mixture and stir, continue to stir in the cheddar cheese, keeping some aside for the tops.

5. Scoop the beef mixture into the peppers, until evenly dispersed. Place in a baking dish, cover with foil and cook for 25-30 minutes. Remove the foil, add remaining cheese on top of each pepper and bake for an additional 5 minutes, or until cheese is melted.

6. Remove from heat and let cool for 5 minutes. Garnish with parsley and enjoy!

Herb Pork Tenderloin

Ingredients:

- 1 ⅓ lb. Pork Tenderloin
- 3 Garlic Cloves, minced
- 1 tsp. Dried Thyme
- 1 tsp. Dried Rosemary
- ½ tsp. Dried Basil
- ½ tsp. Dried Parsley
- ½ tsp. Sea Salt
- ½ tsp. Black Pepper
- 2 tbsp. Olive Oil
- 4 Thyme Sprigs, for garnish

Instructions:

1. To begin, preheat the oven to 425°F. In a bowl combine the following: garlic, thyme, rosemary, basil, parsley, sea salt, and black pepper. Add the olive oil and mix well.
2. Place the pork loin on a baking sheet and marinate the entire loin with the herb mixture until fully coated. Cover with foil and bake for 40-45 minutes, or until cooked through.
3. Remove from oven and let rest for at least 8-10 minutes, then carefully slice the loin into 3/4 inch slices. Place on a dish, garnish with thyme sprigs and serve. Enjoy!

Coconut Crusted Cod

Ingredients:

- 4 Cod Fillets
- 14 oz. Flaked Coconut
- 1 cup Panko Breadcrumbs
- 4 Eggs, beaten
- 1 cup All-purpose Flour
- 2 tsp. Ground Ginger
- ½ tsp. Garlic Powder
- Himalayan Sea Salt
- 1 Lemon

Instructions:

1. To begin, preheat oven to 350°F. Take out 3 medium bowls, in one bowl combine coconut flakes and breadcrumbs. In the second bowl add flour and spices. In the third bowl, add the eggs and beat them.
2. Coat the cod in the flour mixture, then transfer to the eggs, and last the breadcrumbs. Place each coated cod on a baking sheet. Repeat until all fillets are coated.
3. Bake cod for 12-15 minutes, until lightly golden and crispy. Remove from heat and serve with lemon wedges. Enjoy!

Lemon Butter Lobster Tails

Instructions:

1. To begin, use sharp kitchen shears and cut through the top of the shell down to the tail, leaving the tail fan intact. Remove the meat from the shell, keeping it attached at the base and seat the meat on top of the shell. BE CAREFUL, shells can be sharp!

2. In a small bowl, add 1 ½ tbsp. fresh parsley, pressed garlic, dijon mustard, olive oil, lemon juice, and cracked black pepper. Stir until fully mixed. Set aside.

3. Preheat oven to broil on high heat. Place the lobster tails on a baking sheet and divide marinade evenly over the tops of each lobster tail. Additionally, place about 1 tbsp. Butter on each lobster tail cut up in smaller pieces.

4. Place lobster tails in the oven, about 6-8 inches from the top. Broil for about 10-12 minutes or until lobster meat is opaque and cooked through. Remove from oven and serve lobster tails, garnish with leftover parsley and lemon wedges. Enjoy!

Ingredients:

- 4 Lobster Tails (approx. 5 oz. each)
- 2 Garlic Cloves, finely pressed
- 2 tbsp. Olive Oil
- 2 tbsp. Lemon Juice, fresh
- 1 Lemon
- 4 tbsp. Butter
- 1 tsp. Dijon Mustard
- Black Pepper, to taste
- 2 tbsp. Fresh Parsley, chopped

Alfredo Crab Stuffed Shells

Ingredients:

- 12 Dry Jumbo Pasta Shells
- 16 oz. Alfredo Sauce
- 1 large Brown Egg
- 1 lb. small Shrimp (peeled, deveined, no tails)
- 3 oz. pkg. Lump Crabmeat
- 1 ½ cups Ricotta Cheese
- 3/4 cup shredded Parmesan Cheese
- 2 Lemons
- 1 tsp. Parsley
- 1 tbsp. Olive Oil
- Himalayan Sea Salt and Black Pepper

Instructions:

1. To begin, heat a large pot of water with a pinch of sea salt and bring to a boil. Add in the pasta shells and boil uncovered for about 9-10 minutes, stirring occasionally. Drain well.

2. Preheat oven to 350°F. In a large mixing bowl add in the beaten egg, ricotta cheese, parmesan cheese, parsley, and crabmeat. Mix well and set aside. Cut the lemons into wedges and set aside.

3. Heat the olive oil on a large skillet over medium-high heat. Add the shrimp to the skillet and lightly sprinkle salt. Cook shrimp until opaque, about 3-4 minutes. Once cooked, add to the cheese mixture.

4. Spoon the shrimp-cheese mixture into shells, about 2 tbsp. each. Once all shells are filled, heat the alfredo sauce and pour about 1 cup into a baking dish. Arrange the stuffed shells on top of the sauce and spoon remaining sauce evenly across the shells.

5. Cover the baking dish with foil and bake for about 18-20 minutes. Remove the foil and place back in the oven for about 10 minutes. Remove and serve, garnish with parsley and lemon wedges. Enjoy!

Stuffed Chicken Caprese

Ingredients:

- 4 (6 oz.) Chicken Breast Fillets
- ⅓ cup Sun-dried Tomato Oil
- 3 Garlic Cloves, minced
- 2 Roma Tomatoes, sliced
- 12-15 Fresh Basil leaves
- 4 slices Mozzarella Cheese
- ½ cup Mozzarella Cheese, shredded
- 2 tsp. Italian Seasoning
- ⅓ cup Balsamic Vinegar
- Himalayan Sea Salt

Instructions:

1. To begin, preheat the oven to 350°F. Take the chicken breasts and cut each into a pocket of about 3/4 of the way through the side being careful not to cut all the way through. Lightly drizzle the sun-dried tomato oil on each chicken fillet, then season with salt, pepper, and the Italian seasoning.

2. In each pocket, fill the chicken with 2 tomato slices, basil leaves, and mozzarella slice. To seal, use 3-4 toothpicks while cooking to keep contents inside the pocket.

3. In a large skillet over medium-high heat, heat 2 tbsp. Sun-dried tomato oil. Add the chicken and cook on each side for 2-3 minutes or until golden. While cooking, in a mixing bowl add the garlic, balsamic vinegar and a touch of salt. Pour around the chicken breasts in the skillet, bring to a simmer while stirring occasionally. Cook for about 2 minutes or until the sauce has thickened.

4. Top the chicken breasts evenly with the shredded mozzarella cheese and transfer the skillet to the oven for 12-15 minutes, or until the chicken is cooked through.

5. Remove from oven and carefully remove the toothpicks. Serve immediately and top with remaining sauce. Garnish with fresh basil and enjoy!

Classic Pot Roast & Potatoes

Ingredients:

- 1 (3-5 lb.) Chuck Roast
- 4 tbsp. Olive Oil
- 6 Whole Carrots, chopped into ¼ inch thick slices
- 5 Garlic Cloves, minced
- 1 large Yellow Onion, chopped
- 1 lb. small Gold Potatoes (halved or quartered)
- 3 cups Beef Broth
- 1 ¼ Cup Dry Red Wine
- ½ cup Water
- 2 Rosemary Sprigs
- 3 Thyme Sprigs
- 1 tsp. Cumin
- 1 tsp. Sea Salt
- 1 tsp. Black Pepper

Instructions:

1. To begin, preheat the oven to 350°F. Season the chuck roast with sea salt and black pepper all over. In a large skillet over medium-high heat, heat 2 tbsp. olive oil. Once the oil is hot, brown the roast by cooking for 5 minutes on each side. Remove from heat and transfer to a plate.

2. Add the remaining olive oil to the same skillet. Add in the garlic and onions and sauté for 2-3 minutes, until fragrant. Then add the carrots and potatoes. Cook for 6-8 minutes or until they begin to gain color. Add in the beef broth, water, red wine, and cumin. Place 2 rosemary and thyme sprigs atop after mixing and add the pot roast to the center.

3. Cover with lid or foil and cook for 3-3.5 hours, or until tender. Remove from heat and transfer the chuck roast to a cutting board, covered in foil. Let sit for 10-15 minutes, use a fork to break apart into pieces. Serve with the potatoes and carrots on the side, garnish with fresh thyme and rosemary. Enjoy!

Mushroom Beef Stroganoff

Ingredients:

- 1 lb. Ground Beef (Lean)
- 1 Yellow Onion, diced
- 1 lb. Wide Egg Noodles
- 2 tbsp. Fresh Parsley, chopped
- 16 oz. Whole Mushrooms, sliced
- ½ cup Sour Cream
- 2 cups Beef Broth
- 2-3 tbsp. All-purpose Flour
- 2 Garlic Cloves, minced
- 1 tsp. Worcestershire Sauce
- 1 tbsp. Olive Oil
- ½ tsp. Allspice
- 1 tsp. Sea Salt
- 1 tsp. Black Pepper

Instructions:

1. To begin, heat a medium skillet over medium-high heat, add the olive oil, garlic, and onion. Cook for 2-3 minutes, until fragrant. Add in the ground beef and break apart with the spatula. Cook for 8-10 minutes, until no more pink remains. Discard of any excess fat at this time.

2. Add in the mushrooms and continue to cook for 2-3 minutes. Slowly, stir in the flour. Now add the following: beef broth, Worcestershire, allspice, sea salt, and black pepper. Bring to a boil, then reduce the heat to allow to simmer for 8-10 minutes.

3. While the meat simmers, get the egg noodles ready. In a pot, bring water and a pinch of salt to boil. Add in the egg noodles and cook for 10-12 minutes, until al dente. Drain noodles.

4. Remove beef from heat, add in the sour cream, egg noodles, and parsley and stir to mix. Serve in bowls or straight from the skillet and garnish with additional parsley. Enjoy!

Baked Lemon Mustard Chicken

Instructions:

1. To begin, preheat the oven to 350°F. Season the chicken with 1 ½ tbsp. whole grain mustard, salt, and pepper. In a large skillet over medium-high heat, heat the olive oil. Sear the chicken, cooking for 4-5 minutes per side.

2. While the chicken cooks, cut one of the lemons into rounds. In a non-stick baking dish, add lemon rounds to the bottom and transfer chicken on top. In a bowl mix the rest of the whole grain mustard, dijon mustard, honey, and butter. Brush this mixture all over the chicken and pour any remaining liquid into the dish. Place the rosemary sprigs in between the chicken pieces.

3. Bake for 40-45 minutes, or until golden brown and cooked through. Remove and serve straight from the baking dish. Enjoy!

Ingredients:

- 1-2 lbs. Chicken Thighs or Breasts, bone-in
- 1 Lemon
- 3 tbsp. Dijon Mustard
- 3 tbsp. Honey
- 1 tbsp. Olive Oil
- 3 tbsp. Whole Grain Mustard
- 2 tbsp. Butter, melted
- 2-3 fresh Rosemary Sprigs
- 2 Garlic Cloves, minced
- ½ tsp. Sea Salt
- ½ tsp. Black Pepper

Oven Fried Parmesan Chicken Thighs

Instructions:

1. To begin, preheat the oven to 400°F. In a medium mixing bowl, combine the following: parmesan, sea salt, black pepper, paprika, garlic powder, oregano, dill, and parsley. Mix well then add the mayonnaise and mix until smooth.

2. Dip the chicken into the bowl until coated on all sides and then repeat until all chicken thighs are covered. Then in another bowl press the chicken into the breadcrumbs until well coated. Drizzle with olive oil.

3. In a large cast iron skillet over medium-high heat, melt the butter. Add the chicken into the skillet of butter and place in the oven for 30-35 minutes, until golden crispy. Make sure to rotate the chicken halfway through.

4. Remove from oven, transfer to a serving dish and garnish with fresh dill. Enjoy!

Ingredients:

- 1 ¼ lb. Chicken Thighs, skin-on
- ½ cup Mayonnaise
- 5 tbsp. Butter
- 1 cup Panko Breadcrumbs
- ¼ cup grated Parmesan
- ½ tsp. Sea Salt
- ½ tsp. Smoked Paprika
- ½ tsp. Black Pepper
- ½ tsp. Garlic Powder
- ½ tsp. Oregano
- ½ tsp. Dried Dill
- ½ tsp. Dried Parsley
- Fresh Dill, for garnish

Parmesan Chicken with Spaghetti

Ingredients:

- 4 (8 oz.) Chicken Breast
- 1 lb. Spaghetti
- ½ cup Panko Breadcrumbs
- ½ cup Breadcrumbs
- ⅓ cup All-purpose Flour
- ¼ Parmesan Cheese, grated
- 3/4 cup Mozzarella Cheese, shredded
- 2 tbsp. Butter
- 2 Eggs
- 1 tsp. Italian Seasoning
- 1 tsp. Garlic Powder
- 1 cup Marinara
- 3 tbsp. Canola Oil
- 1 tsp fresh Parsley, for garnish
- Himalayan Sea Salt and Black Pepper

Instructions:

1. To begin, preheat the oven to 450°F. While preheating, place the chicken breast between plastic wrap and use a meat mallet to pound to about ¼ inch. Lightly season both sides with garlic powder, sea salt, and black pepper.

2. Heat 6-8 cups of water with a pinch of salt in a large pot, bring to a boil and add in the spaghetti. Cook for 8-12 minutes, stirring occasionally until cooked. Remove from heat and strain.

3. Prepare 3 separate shallow bowls or plates for the following: First bowl, combine the Italian seasoning and flour. Second, add the 2 eggs and beat them until smooth. The third bowl, mix the breadcrumbs and the panko breadcrumbs.

4. One at a time, coat the chicken breast in the flour, then eggs, and lastly in the breadcrumbs. Set aside until all chicken is coated. In a large skillet, heat the canola oil over medium-high heat. Once hot, add the chicken and cook for 2 minutes on each side, until crispy.

5. Transfer the skillet into the oven and bake for 4-6 minutes. Flip the chicken and pour the Marinara on top. Divide the parmesan and mozzarella evenly across each chicken breast. Bake for 5 minutes. Remove from oven, plate on a bed of spaghetti. Garnish with parsley and enjoy!

Classic Clam Chowder

Ingredients:

- 2 (6.5 oz.) Chopped Clams
- 3 cups Milk
- 1 cup Whipping Cream
- 2 Potatoes, peeled
- 3 tbsp. Butter
- 1 small Yellow Onion, diced
- ¼ cup Flour
- Himalayan Sea Salt and Black Pepper
- Parsley, for garnish

Instructions:

1. To begin, get a large pot and heat over medium-low. Add the butter and stir, until melted. Add the onions and cook until translucent, 6-8 minutes. Once cooked, add in the flour and a pinch of salt. Slowly stir the milk and whipping cream, constantly stirring until it comes to a boil.

2. Once the milk is thick, cut up your potatoes into ¼ inch diced pieces and add them. Bring to a simmer for 12-15 minutes, until cooked through.

3. Add the clams, undrained. Let simmer until entire contents are fully heated. Season with salt and pepper, to taste.

4. Transfer to soup bowls, garnish with parsley and enjoy!

Beef Wellington

Ingredients:

- 1-1.5 lb. Beef Tenderloin Fillet
- 2 Eggs, beaten
- 1 tsp. Water
- 3 tbsp. Olive Oil
- 2 Rosemary Sprigs (additional for garnish)
- 7 oz. Puff Pastry
- 10-12 slices Prosciutto
- 2 tbsp. All-purpose Flour
- 1 lb. Cremini or Chestnut Mushrooms
- 2 tbsp. Yellow Mustard
- Sea Salt and Black Pepper, to taste

Instructions:

1. To begin, season the fillet with sea salt and pepper. In a medium skillet over medium-high heat, add the olive oil. Once hot, sear each side of the fillet. Remove from heat and transfer to plate, let cool for 5-10 minutes.

2. Use a brush to cover the fillet in mustard on all sides, then set aside. Chop the mushrooms in half and put them in a food processor to purée. Once puréed, heat the same skillet to medium-high heat and add the mushrooms. Sauté for 6-8 minutes, set aside to cool and mix in the rosemary leaves (discard of stems).

3. Using plastic wrap, 1-2 layers laid out, add the prosciutto until it is long enough to roll the beef tenderloin, then spread the mushrooms on top. Place the tenderloin in the middle and wrap, twist the corners to secure tightly, and refrigerate for 25-30 minutes.

4. Preheat the oven to 400°F. On a floured surface roll out the puff pastry, big enough to wrap the entire fillet. Take the plastic wrap off and transfer to the middle of the puff pastry, roll and fold corners to secure. In a medium bowl, mix the eggs and water until smooth. Brush all over the pastry and let sit for 10 minutes.

5. Transfer the pastry to a baking sheet, brush the top and sides with remaining egg wash, then use a sharp knife to score the top.

6. Bake for 30-35 minutes for medium-rare. Remove from heat, let cool for 10 minutes, then carefully slice 1-inch slices. Garnish with rosemary and enjoy!

Whole Sea Bass

Ingredients:

- 1 Whole Sea Bass (scaled, gills removed and gutted)
- 1 tbsp. Olive Oil
- 1 tsp. Soy Sauce (Low Sodium)
- 2 tsp. Butter, melted
- 1 Lemon
- 2 Thyme Sprigs
- Himalayan Sea salt
- Pink Peppercorn

Instructions:

1. To begin, preheat oven to 425°F. In a small bowl, mix the juice of half the lemon, butter, and soy sauce. Cut the remaining half of lemon into rounds.

2. Take 3-4 lemon rounds and a sprig of thyme to insert them inside the sea bass cavity (middle of the fish). Next, take a large cast iron skillet heat the olive oil over and high heat. Add in the whole sea bass to the middle of the pan and cook for 2-3 minutes on each side.

3. Transfer fish from skillet to a baking sheet. Coat the fish with the butter mixture and season with salt and pink peppercorn. Roast for 7-9 minutes, then finish with the broiler until crispy, 1-2 minutes. Do NOT overcook.

4. Garnish with remaining lemon juice and thyme sprig. Serve with olive oil and herb sauce. Enjoy!

Salmon Chowder

Ingredients:

- 1 ½ lb. Salmon Fillet (skin removed)
- 4 cups Vegetable Stock
- 1 cup Heavy Whipping Cream
- 2 cups Tomato Juice
- 4-5 Russet Potatoes, peeled
- 2 Bay Leaves
- 2 Celery Stalks, chopped
- 2 tbsp. Butter
- 2 tbsp. Thyme
- 2 tbsp. Parsley
- ½ tsp. Cayenne Pepper
- 2 Whole Carrots, peeled and chopped
- Sea Salt and Black Pepper, to taste

Instructions:

1. To begin, prep your salmon and potatoes by cutting them into 1-2 inch pieces.

2. Heat a large pot over medium heat and add the butter. Add in the celery and carrots and cook until tenderized, approx. 5 minutes. Add in the bay leaves, thyme, parsley, a pinch of salt and cook. Stir for about a minute.

3. Add the stock, tomato juice and potatoes and bring to a boil. Reduce heat and simmer for 13-15 minutes.

4. Remove from heat, and slowly stir in the salmon chunks and cream. Keep the heat on medium-low until it is steaming hot. Remove bay leaves and evenly disperse among bowls. Enjoy!

Strawberry Shortcake

Desserts

★★★★★

Blueberry Cobbler

Ingredients:

- 2 pints Fresh Blueberries
- 2/3 cup Whole Milk
- 3/4 cup Sugar
- 1 All-purpose Flour
- 6 tbsp. Butter (individually cut by tbsp.)
- 1 tsp. Sea Salt
- 2 tsp. Baking Powder
- 1 tsp. Vanilla Extract
- 1 tsp. Cinnamon
- 2 tsp. Cornstarch
- 1 tbsp. Lemon Juice
- 2 ½ tbsp. Water

Instructions:

1. To begin, preheat the oven to 400°F. In a large cast-iron skillet, over medium-high heat, melt 3 tbsp. butter. Add the following: blueberries, water, cornstarch, lemon juice, cinnamon, and ½ cup sugar. Stir until the cornstarch begins to dissolve.

2. Bring to a boil, then reduce and let simmer for 3-4 minutes. Remove pan from heat, set aside. In a medium mixing bowl, mix the following: remaining sugar, baking powder, flour, and sea salt. Chop up the remaining butter into smaller pieces.

3. Add the tiny butter pieces into the mixing bowl, along with the milk and vanilla extract. Stir until mixture is smooth and well mixed.

4. Pour the mixture on top of the blueberries, smoothing to cover the entire skillet. Bake for 20-22 minutes, until the top, is lightly golden and the blueberries are starting to bubble over. Remove from heat and let cool for 5-8 minutes, spoon mixture onto plates and serve with homemade vanilla ice cream. Enjoy!

Chocolate Croissants

Ingredients:

- 2 Croissant Dough Sheets, thawed
- 1 Egg, beaten
- 1 tbsp. Water
- 1 lb. Baking Chocolate
- 2 oz. Milk Chocolate, melted
- 2 tbsp. All-purpose Flour
- ¼ cup Butter, melted

Instructions:

1. To begin, preheat the oven to 400°F. Lightly flour the surface and roll out the croissant dough, cutting into triangles. Cut the baking chocolate into 12 even pieces for the filling. Use the melted butter to brush the inside of the croissant, then place a piece of chocolate on each triangle (the widest part).

2. Working from the widest end, roll the dough up to the pointed end and fold. Repeat until all croissants are rolled. In a small bowl, mix the egg and water. Whisk until smooth, then brush over all the croissants.

3. Place the croissants on a greased or non-stick baking sheet, at least 1 inch apart from each other. Bake for 15-17 minutes, until golden crispy.

4. Remove from oven, let cool for 5-8 minutes, while cooling prepare your chocolate. Melt the milk chocolate and transfer to a Ziploc bag. Squeeze into one of the bottom corners of the bag, then cut a tiny corner off to create an opening for the chocolate. Drizzle in your desired pattern on the tops of all croissants. Let sit for 2-3 minutes, then serve. Enjoy!

Strawberry Shortcake

Ingredients:

- 3 ½ cups Fresh Strawberries, sliced
- 1 Lemon
- 4 tbsp. Sugar
- 2 tsp. Baking Powder
- ⅓ tsp. Sea Salt
- ½ tsp. Baking Soda
- ½ cup Milk
- 1 cup All-purpose Flour
- 8 tbsp. Butter
- 8 oz. Whipped Cream
- 1 tbsp. Grand Marnier (optional)
- Fresh Mint, for garnish

Instructions:

1. To begin, preheat the oven to 400°F. In a mixing bowl, combine the following ingredients: 2 tbsp. sugar, baking powder, salt, baking soda and zest of ½ the lemon. Mix well.

2. In a food processor add the butter pieces and process until you have coarse crumbs. Add the butter crumbles and milk, mix until the mixture holds together well. Roll out the dough and cut into 6 biscuits. Place them on a baking sheet and bake for 20-25 minutes, until golden and cooked through.

3. While the biscuits cook, use a food processor to combine the following: ½ cup sliced strawberries, remaining sugar and Grand Marnier. Transfer the strawberry mixture to a large bowl, add the sliced strawberries, mix and let marinate for 25-30 minutes.

4. Remove biscuits from oven and split into halves. Build the shortcake: use the bottom of the biscuit as the bed, add the marinated strawberries, the desired amount of whipped cream and top with the other biscuit half. Garnish with fresh mint, serve and enjoy!

New York Cheesecake

Ingredients:

- 1 ½ cups Graham Cracker Crumbs
- 1 cup Sugar
- 4 Eggs
- 1 tbsp. Lemon Juice
- ½ Lemon Zest
- 1 tsp. Vanilla Extract
- ½ tsp. Cinnamon
- ½ cup Butter, melted
- 3 (8 oz.) pkg. Cream Cheese (room temperature)
- 1 cup Sour Cream
- 1 ½ cups Mixed Berries, for garnish

Instructions:

1. To begin, use a medium-sized mixing bowl to combine the following ingredients: graham cracker crumbs, cinnamon, and butter. Mix well. In an 8 or 9-inch greased baking pan, transfer the crust and press down to form an even layer of crust. Keep refrigerated while preparing the filling.

2. Preheat the oven to 300°F. In another mixing bowl, add the cream cheese and sugar. Mix well then add one egg at a time and beat until well mixed. Add in the vanilla extract, lemon juice, and zest. Mix well, then add the sour cream. Stir to combine, but do not over mix, otherwise filling will begin to grow.

3. Remove the crust from the refrigerator, pour the filling into the crust, use a spoon to make sure it is evenly dispersed. Bake for 75 to 90 minutes, the filling will still move until chilled. Remove from heat, let cool for at least 30 minutes, then transfer to refrigerator for 4-5 hours minimum.

4. Top the cheesecake with fresh mixed berries, slice and enjoy!

Fresh Banana Bread

Ingredients:

- 3 Ripe Bananas, mashed
- ⅓ cup Butter, melted
- 2 tbsp. Butter
- 2 Eggs
- 3/4 cup Sugar
- 2 cups All-purpose Flour
- 1 tsp. Cinnamon
- 1 tsp. Nutmeg
- 2 3/4 tsp. Baking Powder
- ½ tsp. Sea Salt
- 1 tsp. Vanilla Extract
- ½-3/4 cup Walnuts, chopped

Instructions:

1. To begin, preheat the oven to 350°F. In a medium mixing bowl, combine the bananas, eggs, vanilla extract, butter, and ½ cup sugar. Mix well, then add the cinnamon, nutmeg, salt, baking powder, and 1 3/4 cup flour.

2. Mix until completely combined, then add the walnuts. In a non-stick or greased baking pan, pour the mixture and use a spoon to even out.

3. In another mixing bowl, add the remaining flour, butter, and sugar. Beat until it begins to form crumbles. Add the crumbles on top of the banana bread mixture in the pan and then bake for 1 hour. Use a toothpick in the center to make sure there is no batter left.

4. Let cool for 10 minutes, remove from pan and slice!

Chocolate Brownies

Ingredients:

- ¼ cup Unsweetened Chocolate Chips
- ½ cup Semi-Sweet Chocolate Chips
- 1 ⅓ cup Sugar
- ⅓ cup Water
- 2 Eggs, beaten
- ½ cup Vegetable Oil
- 1 tsp. Vanilla Extract
- 3/4-1 cup All-purpose Flour
- ⅓ cup Unsweetened Cocoa Powder
- ½ tsp. Baking Powder
- ½ tsp. Sea Salt
- ½ tsp. Ground Cinnamon

Instructions:

1. To begin, preheat the oven to 375°F. In a small saucepan over medium-low heat, combine the water, sugar, and unsweetened chocolate. Stir and continue to cook, until the chocolate is melted. Sugar will not fully dissolve, once the chocolate is melted remove from heat and let cool for 3-5 minutes.

2. In a large mixing bowl, combine the following ingredients: Cocoa powder, baking powder, chocolate chips, flour, and sea salt. Mix well, then add the eggs, vegetable oil, cinnamon, and vanilla extract. Once mixed, add the melted chocolate and stir only until well combined.

3. Grease an 8x8 pan and pour the chocolate mixture into the pan. Use a spoon to level the top. Bake for 30-40 minutes, you do not want to completely cook so they are moist and chewy. Remove from oven and let cool for 10-15 minutes.

4. Cut the brownies and add vanilla ice cream, if desired. Enjoy!

Lavender Crème Brûlée

Ingredients:

- 3 large Egg Yolks
- 2 ½-3 tbsp. Lavender
- Fresh Lavender Sprigs, for garnish
- ½ cup Milk
- 6-8 tbsp. Baking Sugar
- 2 tbsp. Vanilla Extract
- 1 cup Heavy Whipping Cream

Instructions:

1. To begin, preheat the oven to 250°F. Prepare 6 oven-safe baking dishes on a baking pan. In a small saucepan over medium-high heat, add the milk, heavy cream, and lavender. Bring to a boil, then remove from heat and cover. Allow to sit for at least 30 minutes, this will create the lavender flavor naturally.

2. In a medium mixing bowl, whisk the sugar, vanilla extract, and egg yolks. Reheat the milk, to warm, do NOT make it too hot. Once warmed, add half of the lavender milk to the mixing bowl. Continue whisking and pour the remaining milk.

3. Pour the mixture into each baking dish, until they are all filled evenly. Bake for 50-70 minutes, after 50 minutes if the center is not set by tapping the side of the dish, simply add time until set.

4. Remove from oven and let cool for 30 minutes. Cover each dish with plastic wrap or foil, then refrigerate for 3-4 hours. Sprinkle the baking sugar on top of each dish, to brown the sugar simply use a blowtorch until it begins to caramelize and bubble. Serve immediately and garnish with fresh lavender. Enjoy!

Lemon Poppy Seed Muffins

Ingredients:

- 3/4 cup Sugar
- 6 tbsp. Butter, melted
- 1 Egg
- 1 cup Flour
- ¼ cup Sour Cream
- 1 tsp. Baking Powder
- 1 tsp. Baking Soda
- 1 tsp. Lemon Zest
- 1 ½ tsp. Lemon Juice
- 1 ½ tbsp. Poppy Seeds

Instructions:

1. To begin, preheat the oven to 375°F. In a large mixing bowl, add the sugar, flour, baking powder, baking soda, and lemon zest, and a tiny pinch of salt. Whisk to combine. In a separate bowl, add the melted butter, egg, sour cream, and lemon juice. Whisk as well.

2. Pour the wet mixture into the dry mixture and mix well. Keep mixing while stirring in the poppy seeds. Line a cupcake pan with muffin cup liners.

3. Using a measuring spoon, add about 3/4 batter into each cup liner until all batter has been used. Bake for 20-25 minutes, or until golden brown. Allow to cool for 5 minutes, then serve. Enjoy!

Pumpkin Spice Blondies

Ingredients:

- 3 cups All-purpose Flour
- 3/4 cup Pumpkin Puree
- 1 cup Brown Sugar
- 1 cup Sugar
- 1 cup Butter, melted
- 1 Egg Yolk
- 1 ½ tsp. Vanilla Extract
- 1 tsp. Ground Cinnamon
- 1 tsp. Pumpkin Spice
- ½ tsp. Nutmeg
- 3/4 tsp. Sea Salt
- ¼ tsp. Baking Powder
- Pumpkin Seeds (optional, for garnish)

Instructions:

1. To begin, preheat the oven to 350°F. In a medium-sized mixing bowl, whisk the butter, brown sugar, and regular sugar together. Once well combined, add in the egg yolk, pumpkin puree, and vanilla extract. Keep mixing.

2. In a separate mixing bowl, combine the following ingredients: 2 3/4 cups flour, nutmeg, pumpkin spice, salt, and baking powder. Stir in the dry mixture into the pumpkin mixture, keep stirring until well combined.

3. Prepare a non-stick or greased pan, pour in the mixture and even out with a spoon. In a small bowl, mix about 2-3 tbsp. sugar and the cinnamon together. Sprinkle on the entire mixture.

4. Bake for 20-25 minutes. Remove from oven and let cool for at least 5 minutes. Garnish with pumpkin seeds, if desired. Enjoy!

Snickerdoodle Cookies

Ingredients:

- 3 cups All-purpose Flour
- 1 ½ cup Sugar
- 1 cup Butter, melted
- 1 Large Egg
- 1 ½ tsp. Vanilla Extract
- 1 ½ tsp. Ground Cinnamon
- 1 tsp. Baking Powder
- ¼ tsp. Sea Salt

Instructions:

1. To begin, preheat the oven to 350°F. In a bowl, mix the following ingredients: Flour, baking powder, and sea salt. In a separate bowl, mix the melted butter and 1 ¼ cup sugar. Once fluffy, add in the egg and vanilla. Continue to mix until well combined.

2. Pour in the flour mixture into the butter mixture, continue stirring. Mixture should be nice and smooth, if it is sticking add in 1 tsp. of flour at a time to fix.

3. On a plate, add the remaining sugar and cinnamon together. Lightly mix and set aside. Using a ¼ cup measuring cup or an ice cream scoop, one at a time take out a scoop of dough and roll into a ball. Then roll the ball in the cinnamon sugar and set aside. Repeat until all cookies are rolled and coated.

4. Place the cookie rolls on a greased baking sheet. Bake for 12-15 minutes, do NOT overcook so that it is still chewy. Remove from heat and allow to cool for a few minutes. Serve and enjoy!